Razzle Dazzle! MAGIC TRICKS FOR you

880331-
1990

Larry White and Ray Broekel   Pictures by Meyer Seltzer

Albert Whitman & Company, Niles, Illinois

We dedicate this book to our friend Ray Goulet.
His world-renowned collection of magic books and apparatus
combined with his knowledge and his unbounded friendship
toward all magicians and magicians-to-be
truly makes him today's "magic man" of Boston.
We hope one day you will meet Ray, "magic" will happen,
and you, too, will be under his spell!

Text © 1987 by Laurence B. White and Ray Broekel.
Illustrations © 1987 by Meyer Seltzer.
Published in 1987 by Albert Whitman & Company, Niles, Illinois.
Published simultaneously in Canada
by General Publishing, Limited, Toronto.
All rights reserved. Printed in U.S.A.
10 9 8 7 6 5 4 3 2 1

Library of Congress Cataloging-in-Publication Data

White, Laurence B.
  Razzle dazzle! magic tricks for you .

  Summary: Instructions for twenty easy magic
tricks with an introduction explaining basic magic principles.
  1. Tricks—Juvenile literature. [1. Magic
tricks.] I. Broekel, Ray. II. Seltzer, Meyer, ill. III. Title.
GV1548.W478 1987   793.8   87-6114
ISBN 0-8075-6857-0 (lib. bdg.)

Contents

Know how to make a rope stand straight up?

Hang it from the ceiling.

Getting Started

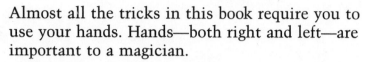

Now for my vanishing frankfurter trick. I call it <u>dog</u> <u>gone</u>.

Almost all the tricks in this book require you to use your hands. Hands—both right and left—are important to a magician.

Several of the tricks depend on your ability with *sleight of hand*. A *sleight* is a secret move, or action, the audience doesn't know happens. In "The Vanishing Cracker" (page 24) you must pretend to place a cracker in one hand while really keeping it hidden in the other. In "Penny-tration" (page 36) you must do the same with a penny.

Misdirection—making people look where you want them to—is an important part of sleight of hand. Suppose you are performing "The Vanishing Cracker." You hold a cracker in your right hand but want your audience to think you are holding it in your left. Pretend to put it in your left hand. Tell your audience this is what you are doing. Then hold your left hand as if it contained the cracker. Stare at your left hand. Don't look at the hand secretly hiding the cracker. An audience will look where you look.

What you say—your *patter*—is also important. Patter can be used to mislead, confuse, or distract an audience. In "Two-Card Fooler" (page 14) you keep mentioning your right and left hands as you move two trick cards back and forth between them, turning the cards with each move. Your audience will be so busy following what you say you are doing that they won't suspect your secret. Patter can also be used to entertain. "Whenever I do this trick, I always have a ball!" you say in performing "A Tube to My Right, a Tube to My

Left" (page 38). Suddenly a bright red ball rolls out the end of a tube and across the table. The best magicians amuse *and* fool their audiences. They are showmen.

Magicians also use *gimmicks*. These are special pieces of equipment that are needed for a trick to work but are kept secret from the audience. In "A Tube to My Right, a Tube to My Left" the gimmick is an unbent paper clip. In "The Mystery of 96" (page 8) a special card with a secret flap is used. *Never* show your audience your gimmick!

Timing—doing or saying the right thing at the right time—is another important tool of magicians. In "Reversing Ribbons" (page 33) a red ribbon and a blue ribbon are placed in separate paper bags. When they are taken out, they appear to have magically changed positions. Your audience will think there is another ribbon in each of the bags. There isn't. You could tear open the bags immediately to show them empty, but with timing—and showmanship—you can have more fun. Stall. Pretend you have been caught. Act embarrassed. Fumble. Then suddenly tear open the bags to show that they are empty. To entertain and fool an audience, magic must be done at exactly the right speed.

Finally, learning to do magic takes *practice*. Practice the different parts of each trick separately *and* together. Practice in front of a mirror. When you are able to fool yourself, you are ready to fool your friends.

5

Over and Under

The Trick

Set two rectangles of paper—one red and one blue—on a table. Arrange them in a *V* shape with the bottom of the red sheet overlapping the bottom of the blue sheet. "Please remember that red is on top of blue," you say. You roll up the papers together, starting at the point of the *V* where they overlap. Stop rolling when only the two top corners are left sticking out.

Now you call upon the help of a spectator. "So I can't roll the papers all the way over, would you press your fingertips on the top corners to hold them in place?" He does this. "Remember," you say, "the papers are arranged with the red on top. You are holding the corners so I can't roll them over. The red will still be on top when I unroll them, right?" "Yes," your helper will agree. You unroll the papers to reveal the blue is now on top of the red. And the helper's fingers are still on the corners!

Here's How

Some magicians do this trick with a one and a five dollar bill. You can if you wish, but two pieces of paper in contrasting colors will show up better. Cut two rectangles about the size of dollar bills (2½ x 6 inches).

You must lay the rectangles down on a table with the lower point of the *V*, where the two colors overlap, toward you. The top of the *V* should be toward the spectator. The paper on your right must always be on top of the paper on your left. If it is not, the trick will fail.

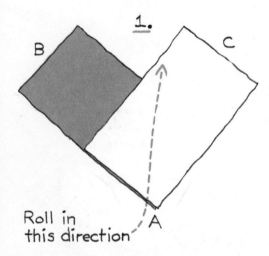

1.

B

C

Roll in this direction

A

2.

Corner B about to flip over... You're doing GREAT!

C

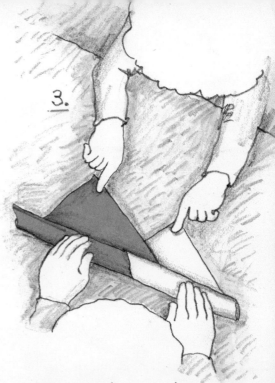

Call attention to the color of the right-hand paper and the fact that it is on top. Then begin to roll up the two papers together, starting at the point of the V (A in the illustration). Now for the tricky part: You must roll the papers slightly toward the right so that the left-hand top of the V (B in the illustration) is reached before the right-hand top of the V (C in the illustration). Keep rolling the papers until end B flips around once. (This will happen *before* the roll reaches C.) As soon as B has made a single flip, stop rolling. The two top ends of the V will extend toward the spectator.

Ask him to press a finger against each of these ends. As he holds onto them, unroll the papers. Because of the secret flip of B, the left sheet will now be on top of the right sheet. You might be tempted to try to roll the papers up again right away and have them go back the way they were. Don't even try. Remember the left-hand rectangle is now on top, and that's wrong. If you try, the papers will not unroll at all.

Now you're ready to unroll!

Truly Amazing!

The Mystery of 96

Glue together

White squares are folded and glued.

Glued white squares are then glued to black square leaving a black border.

The Trick

You hold a card with a large number 6 in your right hand. "You know, it's strange," you say. "When I hold this card in my right hand, I see the number 6. But when I hold the card in my left hand, I see the number 9! Turning the card upside down, you pass it to your left hand. You continue to pass the card back and forth several more times, always turning it upside down as it goes from left hand to right and repeating the patter, "It's a 6 in my right hand and a 9 in my left hand." Then before the audience tires of your joke, you turn the face toward you and bring the card in close to your chest, holding on with both hands. "I've got an interesting idea," you say. "Do you suppose if I hold the card with *both* hands, this might happen?" You flip the card over. A big 96 is now written on it! "No! That could never happen!" you exclaim as you set the card aside and move on quickly to your next trick.

Here's How

Before you can do this trick, you must make a "flap card," a special type of magician's card that can show two different faces on the same side. You will need a heavy piece of black cardboard, two sheets of heavy white paper, some glue, and a thick marking pen. Cut the black cardboard into a square at least twelve inches across (larger for big audiences). Cut the two sheets of white paper into squares the same size as each other and just a bit smaller than the cardboard. (If you lay the papers on the cardboard, you should see about a half-inch border of black around the edge.)

Next, fold the two sheets of white paper in half. Carefully glue the two top halves of the papers together, making sure the edges line up. When the glue is dry, glue the two bottom halves to the cardboard, being careful to leave an even black border around them. You have now made a flap card. It looks like a black card with a white center, but by moving the flap back and forth you can change the sides of the center. On one side, draw a big 6 with the felt marker. Turn the flap over and draw a big 96 on the blank side. To hide the fold down the middle of the paper, make a grid of light pencil lines. The card is finished.

To perform the trick, hold the card in your right hand with the number 6 showing. Use your thumb or fingers to keep the flap closed. To change the 6 to a 9, simply turn the card upside down. Then as you take the card in your left hand, grasp it so that you keep the flap closed. You can repeat this part of the trick several times. Just be sure not to bore your audience with it and to keep the flap closed at all times.

Finally, turn the card over so that the flap faces you and grasp the card with both hands along the sides. As you talk, you can flip the flap over with your thumbs. Once the position of the flap is reversed, adjust the hand that's on the flap side of the card so that the fingers hold the flap closed. Then turn the card over so the 96 shows to the audience.

6 written on flap

96 written on other flap. To hide the fold down the middle of the paper, make a gridwork of light pencil lines.

Right and Left Knots

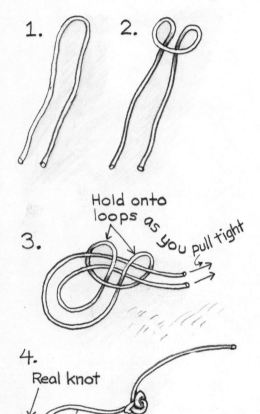

1.

2.

3.

Hold onto loops as you pull tight

4.

Real knot

Vanishing knot

The Trick

You dangle a piece of rope from one hand. The rope has two knots tied in it several inches apart. "Do you realize that knots are left-handed and right-handed, just like people?" you ask. "This is a left-handed knot," you explain, pointing to one of the knots. "And this," you say, pointing to the other, "is right-handed. To prove it, all I have to do is blow on them." You take an end of the rope in each hand and blow hard on the knots. One knot vanishes. You point to the one that remains. "And now everyone can see that this one is left, right?"

Here's How

Obviously this trick is just for fun. One knot is quite ordinary; the other is a special "vanishing knot," which will disappear when you tug hard on the ends of the rope. To tie a vanishing knot, follow the steps shown in the illustrations. Be sure to hold onto the loops as you pull both ends of the rope through them, or the knot will vanish in your hands. Keep trying and you'll soon get the knack. The vanishing knot will look fatter than an ordinary one. Now, a few inches away, tie two ordinary but somewhat loose knots, one on top of the other (to look like the fat, dissolving knot you've just made). You're ready to perform.

As you blow on the vanishing knot, pull hard on the ends, and it will disappear as if by magic. But people probably won't dwell on the mystery; they will be too busy moaning at your terrible pun!

The Trick

Call a friend and ask her to get a penny and a nickel. Tell her to hold one of the coins in her right hand and the other in her left hand without letting you know which hand holds which. Then ask her to do some simple math and to say "Okay" when she has finished with each step. "First multiply the coin in your right hand by 10," you say. You wait until she says "Okay." "Now multiply the coin in your left hand by 13." Again you wait until she lets you know she is done. "Finally add the two totals together and add 5," you say. When your friend says "Okay," you announce, "You are holding the penny in your left hand and the nickel in your right hand." And you're right!

Here's How

The time it takes to do different math problems is the secret behind this trick. Read the directions above again carefully. You must notice how long it takes your friend to complete each step. If she is holding the penny or the nickel in her right hand, she will easily do the multiplication you ask (1 x 10 = 10 or 5 x 10 = 50), so she will answer "Okay" almost immediately. Her left hand is the clue. You ask her to multiply the coin in her left hand by 13. If this hand holds the penny, she will do the multiplication very quickly (1 x 13 = 13). However, if it holds the nickel, it will take her much longer (5 x 13 = 65). Her delay in saying "Okay" is your clue that she is holding the nickel in that hand. Once you know which hand holds which coin, ask your friend to "add 5 to the total" to distract her. But remember: if you try the trick again with her, she now knows what 5 x 13 is.

The Right/ Left Telephone Trick

I did a trick on the phone just yesterday, but no one was watching.

Feeling the Weight of Cards

My, I'm feeling well today. I can tell by feel that I'm holding the Ace of Diamonds.

The Trick

Give a deck of cards to a spectator to examine and shuffle. When she is finished, turn around and ask her to hand the cards to you behind your back. Turning again to face the audience, but still holding the deck out of sight behind your back, you explain, "Do you know that every card in the deck has a different amount of ink on it? It takes more ink to print a nine card than a two. And, surprisingly, red ink is heavier than black ink." As you say "nine," you take a card from behind your back and show the audience. It is a black nine. As you say "two," you remove a black two. And as you say "red ink," you remove a red nine and a red two together. "Of course," you continue, "once you know that ink makes each card a different weight, you can name cards just by holding them in your hand." You remove another card from behind your back and hold it facing the audience. You move your hand up and down as if testing its weight and announce, "This is the Five of Spades." You continue to "weigh" cards and name them and are correct every single time. Then you ask someone in the audience to try the trick, and of course, he can't do it.

Here's How

This trick is actually two different tricks done together. You can use either your right or left hand for the first part, but the second part can only be done with the right hand.

Before beginning, secretly remove four cards from the deck and put them in your rear pocket. The cards are a black nine, a black two, a red nine, and a red two. Make a stack with the black nine on top, the black two second, and the red cards on the bottom. Remember the order.

Have the deck shuffled and given to you behind your back. Then turn to face the audience and begin to talk about the weight of cards. As you talk, remove the stack from your rear pocket and set it on top of the deck (still behind you). You are now ready to pretend to find the black nine and two and the red cards "by their different weights."

You must have practiced the right-handed part of the trick beforehand. Take any single card in your right hand and hold it, face out in front of you with your fingers on top and your thumb on bottom. Squeeze the card just a bit so that it bows in toward your palm. Hold the card slightly to your right and look at it. Then move your hand up and down slightly, as if you were trying to judge its weight. As you do this, twist the card sideways *just a little* toward your left. When you find the right place, you will discover that you can see the marking in the corner, on the lower end by your thumb. Once you've glanced at the marking, turn the card back so that it directly faces the audience and say its name out loud. If you try doing this part of the trick with your left hand, you'll understand why it can't be done; you won't be able to see the number in the corner.

Two-Card Fooler

FOOLED YOU —
the King of Spades
is in my other hand...

By the way, I took
first prize for this at
the magicians' convention
but they made me put
it back.

The Trick

You remove two cards from your pocket and fan them out in your right hand. Show the face of one card and the back of the other to the audience. "I have two cards, and I have two hands," you say. "The cards are the King of Spades and the Ace of Hearts, and my two hands are my right and my left." You turn the cards over to show the second face. "It is your job to try to keep track of all four of these things at the same time."

You flip the cards over several more times. "Now I'll take the King of Spades with my left hand," you say, "and put it behind my back." As you do this, you hold the other card, with its back showing, in your right hand. "Are you paying attention?" you ask. "Which card am I holding in my left hand?" Of course, the audience will guess the King of Spades. You pull your left hand from behind your back and show the Ace of Hearts! You put the Ace, with its face toward the audience, in front of the card in your right hand and fan out the two cards. Then you flip the fan over, showing the King of Spades, and say, "No, the King of Spades was over here. I'll try the trick again, this time with my right hand."

You take the King of Spades in your right hand and put it behind your back. Your left hand holds the other card with its back toward the audience. "Which card is in my right hand?" you ask. Again the audience will guess the King of Spades. You remove your right hand to show the Ace of Hearts! "No, no," you say. You put the Ace back in front

14

of the other card and fan them out in your left hand. Then you flip them over to show the King of Spades. "The King was over here."

Here's How

This is a very old kind of trick that makes use of special cards. You will need four cards and some glue to make them. The four cards can be any values, but two of them should be easy cards to remember, such as a King and an Ace. Glue these two cards back-to-back so the King shows on one side and the Ace shows on the other. Magicians call this a "double-face" card. You also need a "double-back" card. Make one by gluing the faces of any other two cards together. When the glue is dry, you are ready to practice.

Have the cards, one on top of the other, in your pocket. Take them out, still stacked together, and hold them up in your right hand by the bottom edge and fan them out. They look like two ordinary cards, one with its face toward the audience and the other with its back toward the audience. Now if you turn your hand over with the cards still fanned out, the audience will think you are turning over two ordinary cards to show the other face and the other back.

The rest of the trick is easy. By flipping the card held behind your back, you can make sure it never matches the one the audience names. Make the trick look and sound more confusing than it actually is by referring to your right and left hands and by changing the hands you use.

15

Grab Bag

I would like to show you something amazing. Close your eyes and watch me carefully.

The Trick

You stand before your audience holding a clear plastic bag half filled with folded slips of paper. You shake the bag, showing the slips of paper being mixed together. "I've discovered something amazing," you explain. "I've written the name of everyone in this audience on a slip of paper and put the slips in this bag. I can't see whose name is on which slip because I've folded the papers. Now I'm going to reach in twice and take out just a few slips." You reach into the bag and remove a few slips. You give these to someone in the audience. Then you reach into the bag again, remove a few more slips, and give these to another person. You ask the first helper to read off the first group of names you drew. "I told you I would show you something amazing," you say when she is finished. "Would all the right-handed people in this room please raise your hands and keep them raised?" Lots of hands go up. All of the people whose names were just read are raising their hands! Somehow you selected only the names of right-handed people. But the audience will not be too impressed because everyone knows most people are right-handed.

You then ask for only the left-handed people to raise their hands. Let's assume three hands go up. You ask the second helper to read the names on his slips. Amazingly, there are exactly three slips, and each bears the name of one of the left-handers! "And," you continue, "I am left with only right-handed names." You pour the remaining slips onto the table where the audience can open them to discover you're right!

Here's How

You'll need a man's handkerchief, about six feet of rope, and of course, practice. The secret behind this trick is that the rope is not tied to you in any way though it appears to be because of the handkerchief. To practice, you will have to ask someone to tie your wrists together with a handkerchief. Then you can loop a rope between your wrists and stand on the two ends to hold them firmly as you will later ask a spectator to do.

Once the rope is pulled tight against the handkerchief, start to rub your wrists back and forth against each other. Notice that your wrists are also rubbing against the rope and can be used to move it. Keep moving your wrists this way until you have worked a bit of the center of the rope through the handkerchief and up toward your fingers. You only need to work enough rope through the handkerchief so that you can catch it with your fingertips. Now pull with your fingers on this part of the rope until it forms a loop large enough for one of your hands to slip through. Slip the fingertips of either hand through the loop and pull back your hands. The loop will ride down the back of your hand and under the handkerchief. Before you can count to three, it will be completely free.

To escape, work rope through center of handkerchief toward fingers until you've formed a loop.

Slip hand through this loop and you're free!

This is not only a magic rope, but I can use it when I take a bath... It's my bathrope.

19

Fastest Knot in the World

The Trick

Holding a single piece of rope, one end in each hand, you ask the audience if they would like to see you tie the fastest knot in the world. Before they have time to respond, you bring your hands together, then separate them. A knot is tied in the center of the rope! "Would you like to see me do it again?" you ask.

Here's How

Use a soft piece of rope about three feet in length. Ordinary clothesline will work well, but if it is stiff, wash it. Let it soak for an hour and then dry it. A piece of brightly colored "jump rope" looks more magical than plain rope.

Hold the rope exactly as shown in the first illustration. Your palms should be facing you. The rope is held between your hands. About six inches of the ends of the rope dangle over your hands. One end hangs over the back of your left hand; the other end over the front of your right hand. This is important. It's how the trick works.

As you bring your hands together, slide your right hand behind your left hand. As you do, open the first two fingers on each hand and let the ends of the rope slip between your opened fingers. Close

Your left hand

Your right hand

your fingers to grip the ends of the rope. The right-hand fingers grasp the end of the rope in the left hand, and the left-hand fingers grasp the end of the rope in the right hand as shown in the second illustration.

Squeeze the ends of the rope tightly with the fingers of both hands and draw your hands apart. Your right hand should pull to the right, and your left hand should pull to the left. A knot will automatically form in the center of the rope.

As you practice, you will find your hands seem to tie the knot by themselves and you can concentrate on speeding up. The quicker you can tie the knot, the more amazing the trick will appear. Be sure you can do the trick smoothly and quickly before you show your friends.

Ends of rope are clipped between 1st and 2nd fingertips on each hand.

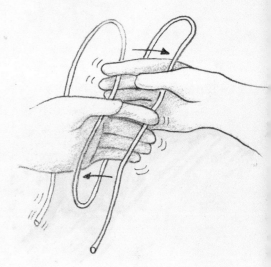

Then right hand pulls to right and left hand pulls to left.

The Great Clock Trick

Please applaud when I finish this trick Save the tomatoes and eggs for the salad... Seriously, it's hard work being the world's greatest magician.

The Trick

You hold up a large square of cardboard with the face of a clock drawn on it. In your other hand, you hold a magic wand. Turning toward a member of the audience, you say, "There are twelve numbers on the face of a clock. Would you please select any one of them? Don't say the number out loud." You turn the face of the clock toward yourself. "Let me see if I can find your number with the help of my magic wand. I'll try to do it by tapping up to the number 20 on the face of the clock. I would like to begin with your number, but I do not know that, and I don't want you to say it. I will need you to help me. When I tap the first time, I would like you to silently begin counting with me, but I want you to start with the next higher number to the one you chose and continue counting my taps until you reach the number 20. Then say 'Stop.' For example, if you are thinking of 3, my first tap would be on your count of 4, my second would be on your count of 5, and so forth, with my last tap being on your count of 20. Then you would say 'Stop.'"

When the spectator understands, you begin tapping. Finally the spectator says "Stop." "I have stopped when you told me to," you say. "My wand now rests on a number." You slowly begin to turn the clock face toward the audience. As you do so, you hold the wand steady on the number you ended with. "What number did you choose?" you ask. The spectator says "10." The clock face is now seen by the audience. The wand rests on 10 o'clock! What's more, you can do the trick again, immediately, with a different number and a different spectator, and it will still work.

Here's How

First you must draw a clock face on a square of cardboard. The face can be simple or fancy; just be sure the numbers are easy to read. The clock should have no hands. You'll also need a pencil or "magic wand" to tap with.

Follow the patter suggested under "The Trick" section to give directions to the spectator. Be certain she understands she must begin to count your taps silently, starting with the next higher number to the one she is thinking of. Also, be sure she understands she is to stop you when she reaches the count of 20 (because at that time you will be pointing to her number). When she thoroughly understands what she is expected to do, you are ready to begin tapping.

Here's the simple secret. You count, too, except you begin on 1 and tap any numbers on the clock face in any direction and any order *until* you count your seventh tap. Your eighth tap *must* be on 12 o'clock. Then forget about counting and just tap to the left (11, 10, 9, 8 . . .) until you are told to stop. Your wand will then be resting on the spectator's number! You can do the trick over and over again. Just make sure that your eighth tap is on 12 o'clock and that you tap to the left after this. And be sure to turn the clock to face the audience carefully so no one thinks you move the wand to the number after the spectator says it.

"Bread, Bread," cried the magician...

And the curtain came down with a roll.

The Vanishing Cracker

The Trick

You hold up a plain cracker with one hand, then place it in your other hand and make a fist around the cracker. "First I put the cracker in this hand," you say. You reach into your pocket with your free hand. "Then I take some magic dust and sprinkle it over the cracker." You squeeze the hand holding the "magic dust" a few times as a crunching, grinding noise is heard. Then your hand opens so the "dust" sprinkles over the fist holding the cracker. "And the cracker vanishes!" you say. You open your closed fist, and the cracker is gone.

Here's How

The trick is just a joke. It will probably only fool people for a moment, but it will make them laugh. To do it, you must perform a magician's "move." (A move is a secret action the audience doesn't know happens.) You must pretend to place a cracker in one hand while really keeping it hidden in the other hand. For the purposes of this explanation, the hand you hide the cracker in at the beginning will be called your "cracker hand." You will need to wear pants or a skirt with a pocket on the same side as this hand. Be sure to use a thin, easy-to-crumble cracker. Follow the steps shown in the illustrations. When the fingers of the empty hand close around the pretend cracker, take your cracker hand away, still upside-down and still holding the cracker. This is an important moment. You must remember that

① Show cracker to audience. Cracker rests over center of middle fingers.

② Hold other hand, palm up, next to cracker hand.

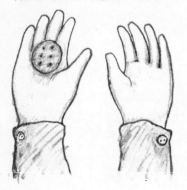

your spectators think the cracker is now in your other hand. Help them continue to think this. Keep that hand closed as though it really did hold the cracker. Look at your closed fist. Never look at the hand secretly hiding the cracker. People will look where you look, so you must look where you want them to look! Magicians call this technique "misdirection."

As you stare at your closed fist, let your cracker hand hang by your side for just a moment. Do not close your cracker hand in a fist: just press the cracker against your open fingers with your thumb and keep the back of this hand toward the audience. Then reach into your pocket with your cracker hand and pretend to get some "magic dust." Of course, all you do is bring out the same cracker, still hidden. Hold this hand over your closed fist. Crunch up the cracker and allow the "dust" to fall over the fist. Do this quickly, then open your fist to show the cracker is gone. How well you fool people will depend on how good you are at convincing them you really did put the cracker into your fist. Practice the move again and again in front of a mirror to learn to do it well.

Turn cracker hand upside-down over free hand while thumb holds on to cracker.

Fingers of free hand curl around "pretend" cracker and cracker hand is taken away.

I'd like to thank my assistant, Ms. Direction, who made this trick possible.

You did it... you clean up. I'm not getting blamed for this!

The Right Tea

The Trick

Holding up your empty left hand, you say, "Some people are lefties." You lower your left hand and hold up your empty right hand. "And some people are righties. Which are you?" The spectator says she is a righty. "Hold out your right hand," you tell her. "Ah yes," you then say. "I can tell right away." You suddenly press your hand down on hers. "The right-tea shows up every time!" As you lift your hand, a bag of tea appears in the spectator's right hand.

Here's How

You must practice misdirection to do this easy and surprising trick. To prepare, take a bag of tea and put a staple in it near the top. Open one side of the staple and bend it down to make a little hook. You must wear a dress or a pair of pants with a hip pocket. Hook the staple over the edge of the pocket so the tea bag hangs down on the outside. The bag will not show to anyone standing in front of you. (It would be a good idea to remove the string and label from the tea bag before performing.)

Begin by showing your hands empty and using the patter described above. Don't mention directly that your hands are empty. As you lower your left hand to your side, hold up your right hand, fingers spread and palm open. Stare at this hand. Don't look at your left hand. Everyone else will look where you are looking. No one will notice as you

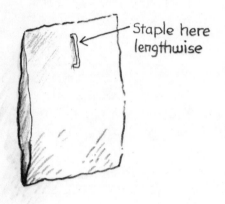

Staple here lengthwise

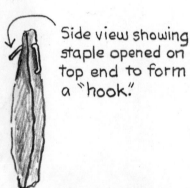

Side view showing staple opened on top end to form a "hook."

move your left hand behind your back and pick off the tea bag, then move your left hand back to where it was. Keep looking at your right hand as you ask whether your spectator is right- or left-handed.

Lower your right hand as you tell the spectator to hold out her right hand (or left, if she is a lefty). Then simply place your left hand—with the tea bag— down over her extended hand. If she is left-handed, just say, "I knew you were because I have some tea left!"

A really tea-rific tearick... Tea-hee

Which Hand Holds Which?

The Trick

Hand a friend a penny and a dime and turn your back. "You have a right hand and a left hand," you say. "Please hold one of the coins in each of your hands and make both hands into fists so I can't possibly see which hand holds which coin." When your friend has done this, ask him to multiply to himself the coin in his right hand by 2, 4, or 6. (He can choose the number.) When he has finished, ask him to multiply the coin in his left hand by 1, 3, or 5. Now ask your friend to add the two answers together and give you the total. Let's say it is 23. "You are holding the dime in your right hand and the penny in your left!" you announce. And you are absolutely correct!

Actually my best trick is called "The Vanishing Money"... I perform it at the candy store.

Here's How

Numbers can be either even (2, 4, 6 . . .) or odd (1, 3, 5 . . .). That is the secret of this trick. A penny is 1 cent, or odd. A dime is 10 cents, or even.

First you ask for the coin in the right hand to be multiplied by 2, 4, or 6—all even numbers. No matter which coin is in this hand, the answer will be an even number. (Penny: $1 \times 2 = 2$, $1 \times 4 = 4$, $1 \times 6 = 6$. Dime: $10 \times 2 = 20$, $10 \times 4 = 40$, $10 \times 6 = 60$.) Because all of the possible answers are even, the right hand is not important to you. But the left hand is!

You ask for the coin in the left hand to be multiplied by 1, 3, or 5—all odd numbers. Suppose the left hand holds the penny. All answers will then be odd ($1 \times 1 = 1$, $1 \times 3 = 3$, $1 \times 5 = 5$). But if it holds the dime, all answers will be even ($10 \times 1 = 10$, $10 \times 3 = 30$, $10 \times 5 = 50$). When the two totals are added together, the grand total that is given to you will be either even or odd depending on which coin the left hand holds. If the total you receive is odd, the left hand holds the penny. If the total is even, the left hand holds the dime.

I'm just waiting for Hollywood to call. I think there was an agent in the audience.

Strange Vibrations

The Trick

You give a friend a deck of cards to shuffle. Taking them back, you glance through the faces of the cards and remove two cards saying, "I feel strange vibrations about these cards." You lay them both side by side, facedown, on the table. Then you hand the deck to your friend and ask her to deal the cards into two separate piles, placing the first card to the left, the second to the right, the third to the left, the fourth to the right, and so on. As she deals, you ask her to stop anytime she wishes. When she does, you invite her to add or subtract cards from the tops of the piles (as many or as few as she likes just so long as she leaves the two bottom cards).

"Now for the mysterious part of this trick," you explain. "Will you press your left hand on the left-hand pile you made?" Your helper does this. You then ask her to pass her left hand over the two cards you set out at the start. As she does, you suddenly say, "Stop! That card [the one her hand is over] is sending out strong *left* vibrations. Please move it over in front of your left pile." She does. You ask her to move the other card, still facedown, before the right-hand pile. "Please turn over both of the piles you made," you then say. Your helper turns the piles faceup to reveal the cards on the bottom of each pile. Let's say they are the Three of Diamonds and the King of Spades.

"I told you I had strange vibrations before we began," you say. "And your left hand also gave me strange vibrations as you passed it over my cards.

Let me show you why." You flip over a Three of Hearts in front of the Three of Diamonds. Flipping over the other card in front of the pile with the King of Spades, you discover it is the King of Clubs! Your "vibrations" have somehow helped you discover the mates of both cards selected by the helper. And the amazing thing about this trick is that your friend can shuffle the cards right then and you can do it again with equal success, even though the cards are different.

Here's How

This impressive trick is amazingly easy to do. When you look through the deck to select your cards "from their vibrations," simply look at the two cards on top of the deck and remember them. If you follow the instructions, these will become the bottom cards of the two piles your helper deals. Whatever these two cards are, you must remove two mates to them. Put these two mates side by side and facedown on the table. (To help you remember which card is which, put the card that matches the top card of the deck on your left. Put the other card to the right of this.) Be a showman; explain that these cards are sending off strange and unusual vibrations. Hand the deck back to your helper.

Remember, you already know the two top cards in the deck. You now ask your helper to deal all of the cards into two piles, starting with a pile on her left. When she does, the top card becomes the bottom card of her left pile (This matches the card

I feel strange vibrations about these two cards.

Ooops, sorry! I washed my hands this morning and now I can't do a thing with them.

on your left) and the second card becomes the bottom card of her right pile! It does not matter how many cards she deals on top. In fact, you can have fun by asking her to add and subtract cards. "Are you sure you have enough on each pile?" you can ask.

Now tell your helper to pass her left hand over the two cards you selected. (This is just to make the trick look more mysterious.) Make sure you feel the "left vibrations" when her hand is over the mate for the card you know is on the bottom of her left-hand pile. Now the trick is practically done. Have your helper turn over her piles to show the bottom cards, and you turn over your two cards. You can repeat the trick immediately, if you like, because after the deck has been shuffled again, there will be two new top cards!

The Trick

Hold up two ribbons, one red and the other blue. Put them each in a small paper bag and set the bags on a table. The bag with the red ribbon should go on the right and the bag with the blue ribbon on the left. "Ladies and gentlemen," you announce, "I am going to make the red ribbon in the bag on the right jump invisibly into the bag on the left, and at the same time cause the blue ribbon in the bag on the left to jump invisibly into the bag on the right." You bring the two bags together, twirl them around to change their positions, and set them back on the table. Then you pull out a bit of ribbon from each bag to show the red ribbon is now in the left-hand bag and the blue is in the right-hand bag. The audience knows, of course, that you simply changed the positions of the bags.

"Now," you continue, "I will make the ribbons again change places and return to their original bags." The audience expects you to do the same thing again, but you fool them. "Please remember the red ribbon is here on the left," you say. You point to the end of the red ribbon extending out, then push it inside. "And the blue ribbon is here on the right." You push the end of the blue ribbon inside the right-hand bag. "Red-go, blue-go, both-go!" you chant as you wave your hands above the bags. "There! It is done!" you announce. "Without touching the bags or the ribbons, I have made the ribbons change places." And you prove it. You take out the red ribbon from the right-hand bag and the blue ribbon from the left-hand bag.

Reversing Ribbons

After the show let's go for some ice cream.

Sorry I can't, I'm wrapping presents.

Sorry you're going to be tied up. Maybe next week.

But the audience is still suspicious. It thinks you must have had two ribbons, a red and a blue one, in each bag. You pretend you've been caught. Then you tear both bags apart and show them empty.

Here's How

Believe it or not, you use only a red ribbon, a blue ribbon, and two small paper bags for this trick. But the ribbons must be specially prepared. Obtain two pieces of colored ribbon, each about two feet in length. They may be any colors but they must be different enough for the audience to remember. The ribbons should be the same widths. Cut three inches off the end of each one. Attach these to the ends of the opposite colored ribbons. You may glue, tape, or sew them on. Just be sure they are firmly attached. When you're done, the red ribbon should have a three-inch blue end and the blue ribbon should have a three-inch red end.

To begin, hold up the two lengths of ribbon with the short colored ends hidden in your hands. Then drop a ribbon into each bag. Set the bag with the red ribbon down on the right and the bag with the blue ribbon on the left. Immediately draw out a short length (about two inches) of the real end of each ribbon and allow it to hang over the edge of the bag. Remind the audience which bag has which ribbon.

Push the ends of the ribbons into the bags and say you will cause the ribbons to change places. Pick up both bags and bring them together. Twirl them

34

around a few times so the audience is not sure which bag contains which ribbon. You must now set the bags down where they were.

Tell the audience the ribbons have changed places. Reach into each bag and draw out two inches of the short "wrong color" ends. Of course, the audience will not be surprised because they'll think you just changed the positions of the bags. Now you are set for the amazing ending. Push the fake ends down inside the bags, wave your hands, and utter your magic words. Then reach into the bags and draw out the ribbons with the short ends hidden in your hands. The ribbons appear to have magically changed positions. And the bags are empty!

Sounds good to me. Get ready— here comes our big number!

Penny-tration

The Trick

"I'd like to show you a famous magic trick that was performed by the great Houdini," you say. You hold up a napkin. "Pretend this is the stage." You set the napkin down on a table and reach into your pocket to remove a playing card. "And this is the solid brick wall that was set up on stage." You lay the playing card down on top of the napkin. "Houdini stood between the audience and the wall. Pretend this penny is Houdini." You take a penny out of your pocket and toss it on the table so your audience can see it. Then you pick it up and hold it, concealed, in your fist. Suddenly you slap your hand down on top of the card. "A screen hid him from view just as my hand is now hiding the penny. When the screen was removed, Houdini had accomplished the impossible." You lift your hand and the penny has vanished. When you lift the card, it is discovered underneath. "Houdini walked right through a solid brick wall!"

Here's How

This trick is an example of a "penetration," a type of magic trick in which one solid object appears to pass through another solid object. A napkin, a playing card, two pennies, and a costume with two hip pockets (one on the right and one on the left) are all you need. Put a penny and the card in one pocket. Put the extra penny in your opposite pocket. Because sleight of hand is involved, you should practice carefully before performing.

Begin by placing the napkin on the table. Next reach into your pocket and remove the card and the penny. You should do this in a special way. Grasp the card at the bottom with your thumb on one side and your fingers on the other. The penny should be hidden between the card and your fingers. You should be able to turn your hand and show the card from both sides without anyone seeing the penny. Finally, set the card down on the napkin so that the penny is underneath the card and on top of the napkin. The napkin will stop the penny from making a sound. Take your hand away.

Now remove the other penny from your opposite pocket and toss it on the table. When the audience has seen it, pick it up in your favorite hand, right or left, whichever you would naturally pick up a coin with, and pretend to place it in your other hand (really keeping it in your first hand). To do this "move," read the instructions for the "The Vanishing Cracker." The action is the same except this time you are using a penny instead of a cracker. Hold the fist the audience thinks contains the penny but doesn't over the playing card. Let your other hand, which really contains the penny, hang by your side close to your pocket. Slap your fist down on the card and then slowly lift and open it to show the penny is gone.

Now turn over the card to show the penny underneath, all the while keeping your eyes on the card. At the same time, drop the hidden penny into your pocket.

Hold coin between fingertips and card; thumb goes on other side.

A Tube to My Right, a Tube to My Left

Straighten paper clip leaving hook on one end.

Genuine 100% magic paper clip

The Trick

Two decorated tubes are on the table before you. The tubes are different colors, and one is thinner than the other. You point to the thick one. "This is the tube to my right," you say. You point to the thin one. "And this is the tube to my left." You pick up the tube on your left and tip it toward the audience saying, "You will notice that the tube to my left is empty and, because it is thinner, the tube to my right will drop right over it." You set the thin tube back down on the table, pick up the thick tube, and slip it over the thin tube. You reach into the top of the nested tubes and remove the thin one, setting it back down on the table to your right. You then pick up the thick tube and tilt it toward the audience to show the insides. "And you will notice that the other tube is also quite empty." You set it back on the table, to your left. "Believe it or not," you say, "I made the tube to my left become the tube to my right! And the tube to my right became the tube to my left!" Your audience is not fooled and may even snicker at your feeble joke. You continue, paying no attention, by picking up the thin tube, which is now on your right.

"This time it is the tube to my right that fits inside the tube to the left," you say. You drop the thin tube into the fat one and push the two nested tubes to the center of the table. "Just like that, before your very eyes, I've fooled you again! I've made the tube to my left vanish, and the tube to my right vanish, and a brand new tube appear—the tube to my middle!" Now the audience really thinks you're a lousy magician. They may even give you a "boo," but bravely you continue.

"This is my favorite trick," you say. "Do you know why?" Without waiting for an answer you lift both tubes together. "Because whenever I do it, I always have a ball!" A bright red rubber ball appears and rolls across the table, leaving your audience totally surprised and truly baffled.

Here's How

Four objects are required for this trick: two tubes made from tin cans with tops and bottoms removed, a bright red rubber ball, and a medium-size paper clip. One of the tubes must be thin enough to fit easily inside the other. The thin tube should be the same height as the thick one. To make them look more magical, decorate them by gluing on patterned, colored paper. (Make each tube a different color so the audience can easily tell them apart.) The ball should be a bright color like red so it stands out and small enough to fit loosely inside the thin tube. Straighten the paper clip as much as possible, leaving a hook on one end. Push the straightened end into the rubber ball. Set the thick tube down on your right and hang the ball inside it by hooking the clip over the rim. Put the paper clip on the side of the tube that's away from the audience, and cover it with your fingers or thumb when you lift the tube. (The colored paper you glued on the tubes will also help camouflage it.) Place the empty, thin tube to your left and you are ready to perform the trick as described above.

When the thick tube (right) is dropped over the thin tube, the ball will go inside the thin tube and the hook will be over the rims of both tubes. (If

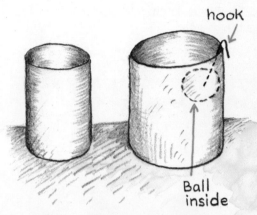

Thick tube on right with ball hung inside on straightened end of paper clip. Thin tube on left.

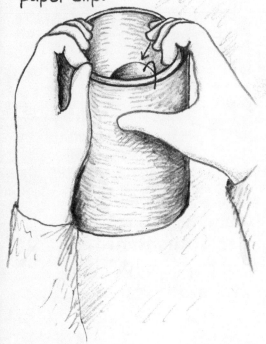

Lift tubes and use fingers to push the ball free from the paper clip.

the ball catches on the top edge of the thin tube, try pushing against the outside of the hook to reposition the ball.) When you pull the thin tube out the top of the thick tube, the ball will automatically be inside the thin tube, which the audience saw empty only a few moments before. Now you can show the thick tube empty. Pick up the thick tube, tilt it toward the audience, and set it back down on your left. You have accomplished two things: you have shown the insides of *both* tubes empty and you have exchanged the positions of the tubes.

When you're ready to do the last part of the trick, simply pick up the thin tube and drop it back inside the thick one. The ball goes with it. Move the nested tubes to the center of the table. Lift the two nested tubes, using both hands. Hold your thumbs on the outside of the tubes near the top and slip your fingers inside to lift them. As you do, you will find your fingers can push the ball free from the paper clip.

The Trick

Fan out a deck of cards and ask a spectator to pick one of them. Then have him return the card to the top of the deck and cut the deck to lose his card. Now glance through the deck and remove a number of cards. Place each, in turn, facedown on the table. Act like you're trying desperately to find the chosen card. "I'm very confused today," you say. "I've been doing so many card tricks, I can't remember which card is which. I'm sure your card is one of these." You point to the pile of cards you have just made. "Will you help me find it?" When the spectator agrees, you sit back and simply give him instructions. "Pick up my pile of cards," you begin. You ask him to deal the cards, one at a time into two piles, one to the right, the other to the left. When he has dealt all the cards, you say, "Now name either pile, right or left." If he chooses the right one, you push that pile to one side and ask him to pick up the remaining pile and again deal it into two piles, right and left.

When the cards have been dealt, you say, "You chose 'right' before, so we will again eliminate the right pile." You push the cards in the new right pile aside to join the already discarded cards. Again you ask the helper to deal the remaining pile into two piles and again you discard the right pile. You repeat this action two more times. Finally there is only one card in each pile, and you again discard the right one, leaving a single card in the left pile. "What was your card?" you ask. You turn over the card that is left, to show the card your helper has just named.

The Help-Me Card Trick

Will you please shuffle this card? Thank you. I need your help in doing this trick. In fact, I need lots of help.

Here's How

There are three steps to this trick. Learn them one by one.

Step 1: You must know what card the helper selected. The easiest way to do this is to glance at the bottom card of the deck and remember it. Ask the helper to return the card he has chosen to the *top* of the deck. Then ask him to cut (not shuffle) the cards. This will put the card you glanced at on top of his card. Now you look through the deck for his card. Pretend to have difficulty finding it. Actually look for the card you glanced at. You know his card is the card right in front of it.

Step 2: You must make a stack of exactly eighteen cards on the table, with the helper's card on top of the stack. The easiest way to do this is to pretend to find his card eighteen times. Do this quickly. Put the cards facedown in a stack on the table. All the while, you are counting. When you have put seventeen cards on the table, remove his card and put it on top. Set the deck aside.

Step 3: Now have the helper deal the pile you have just made into two separate piles, one card at a time. Remember that the first card he deals (the top card) will be the card he chose. This card will be the start of either the right or left pile, depending on which direction he deals. Remember which it is. When all the cards have been dealt into two piles, you must direct the helper to choose the pile with his card. Assume his card is in the left pile. You say, "We have two piles, right and left. Name either one." If he says "left," you say, "Fine, then we will get rid of the right pile." But if he says "right," you say, "Fine, then we will not use the right pile." If his card is in the right pile, say and do the reverse. It does not matter which pile he chooses. You direct him to discard the other one.

The trick is now over for you. Just have him repeat the action until only one pile with one card is left. Discard the same pile each time and remember to use exactly eighteen cards. If you try it with any other number, you will probably discard the helper's card.

WOOPS!

Back to the book!

Can or Can't Cut

Have you ever seen a magician place his assistant in a box and saw her in half without actually hurting her? He does that by hypnotizing her, just as I have hypnotized this ribbon...

The Trick

You display three objects: a short length of ribbon, an envelope, and a pair of scissors. You hand a spectator the ribbon. "This ribbon is under my spell," you say. "I have hypnotized it." You pick up the envelope, seal it, and cut off both ends to produce a tube. "Have you ever seen a magician place his assistant in a box and saw her in half without hurting her?" You take the ribbon and thread it through the envelope so it hangs out each end. "Pretend this envelope is the box, the ribbon is the assistant, and these scissors are the saw. I will just saw the box in half like this." And with that you snip the envelope in two. "Of course, the lady wasn't cut because she was hypnotized." You draw the ribbon out and it is still in one length even though the envelope is now in two pieces. You hand the scissors, half the envelope, and the ribbon to a spectator saying, "Here, you try it." But when he does, he cuts the envelope and the ribbon into two pieces. You explain that he forgot to "hypnotize" the ribbon first and pretend to hypnotize it. Then you do the trick again, yourself, successfully.

Here's How

The secret of this trick is the scissors. Most of the scissors in the world are right-handed. They are made to cut when held in the right hand. If you hold a pair of right-handed scissors in your left hand and try to cut with them, you will have trouble. Try it. Most right-handed scissors held in the left hand will cut the stiff paper that envelopes are made of but *not* soft cloth ribbon. You should only do the trick for right-handed people. Lefties will have had enough frustrating experiences with right-handed scissors to figure it out.

To perform, cut off the ends of a stiff envelope, then thread a soft ribbon through it. Keep the ribbon at the top of the envelope. Hold the scissors in your left hand and snip through the middle of the envelope. You will cut the envelope in half, but the ribbon will remain whole! (If you fail to cut the very top of the envelope, tear it with your hands as you pull the two ends apart to show the ribbon.)

This trick may not work for you the first time you attempt it. You may have to try a few different envelopes, kinds of ribbon, and scissors before you find the ones that work best. Cloth ribbon is usually the best, but plastic ribbon can work as well. Never use paper ribbon. Sometimes loosening the scissors will help. (Use a screwdriver to loosen the screw at the hinge just a bit; if you loosen it too much, the scissors won't even cut the envelope.) Practice holding the scissors naturally in your left hand before performing the trick, so you won't call attention to yourself. And be prepared for what to do in case the trick fails. "Oh, I'm glad I wasn't sawing a person in half!" you can say. "I'm afraid I had better go back to hypnotizing school!" Or, "Sorry, I guess this ribbon forgot how to do the trick!" Then move on to your next "miracle."

The Last Straw

You may not believe me but most people can recognize a right- or left-handed straw when they see one...

We believe you sir... we believe you!

The Trick

"Just like people, drinking straws are right- and left-handed," you say. You hold up a half dozen plastic straws in your fist for your audience to see. Of course, the straws will all look the same to them. "You may not believe me, but most people can easily recognize a right- or left-handed drinking straw when they see one," you say. You fan the straws out in front of one member of the audience. Then you ask her to pick out a right-handed straw and to point to the one she chooses. As she points to a straw, you pull it from your fist. Then you look it over carefully and hand it to her, saying, "Yes, indeed, you are correct. That is a right-handed straw."

You continue to do this with different spectators, always asking them to select a right-handed straw and always telling them they chose correctly. After five straws have been selected, one straw remains in your fist. The spectators will think you are just kidding. But you fool them. "You may wonder how I knew all of the straws you chose were right-handed," you say. "Well, I knew this would be the only one left!" The audience laughs at your joke. But then you slowly open your fist to show the last straw with a tag tightly tied around it. The tag reads: "This is the one that is left."

Here's How

You will need six ordinary plastic drinking straws and a tiny label with "This is the one that is left" clearly printed on it. A hole needs to be punched in one end of the label. You will also need a piece of thin, white elastic thread (the thinnest you can buy) to tie the label on the straw. It should look like heavy sewing thread. Pass the elastic through the hole in the label and tie it around one straw. (Tie it tight enough so it stays in place but do not stretch the elastic.) This straw now looks like it has a label tied to it with a piece of string. But you can push the tip of a pencil into the loop to stretch it open. While it is open, push the other straws into the loop one by one. You now have the label tied around all of the straws. Slide the string about a third of the way up from the bottom of the bundle and grasp the bundle in your hand. Because the label is hidden inside your fist, it looks as though you are simply holding a bunch of straws.

Fan the straws out and allow one to be selected. Pull this straw free from your fist. The label, of course, stays hidden in your fist around the remaining straws. Each time a straw is selected, the label stays around the remaining straws and the loop gets smaller.

Finally, the loop is left in your fist tightly tied to the last straw. When you open your hand, the straw that is left displays the label tied on with an innocent-looking piece of thread. Let your audience read, but not touch, the label and thread. If they gave the thread a tug, your secret could be discovered.

And now for the finale... I will cast a magic spell. Hold your breath and raise your right arm. Now also lift your right leg and your left arm... Now raise your left leg!

OK... what do I do now?

Goodbye... You've been great. Hope you liked the show.

About the Authors

Larry White started doing magic tricks when he was in first grade. He was soon earning his spending money by putting on magic shows. Today he wishes he still had all the money he earned from his childhood performances.

Author of many science and magic books for children, Larry White serves as the Director of the Science Center for the Needham, Massachusetts, schools. He and his wife, Doris, and their two sons, Bill and Dave, live in Stoughton, Massachusetts.

Ray Broekel has written and edited around two hundred books and one thousand articles and stories, most of them for children. Dr. Broekel is considered to be the #1 authority in the United States on the history of chocolate and candy bars. One of his favorite tricks is to make a chocolate candy bar disappear.

Ray Broekel lives with his wife in Ipswich, Massachusetts. They have two grown children and also grandchildren.

and Illustrator

Meyer Seltzer has been proving that the hand can fool the eye ever since his graduation from the School of the Art Institute of Chicago. In the field of magic he is skilled in being a good audience and is *always* amazed. He has illustrated many books and received awards too numerous and inconsequential to list.